Dress Better Feel Better

Elevate Your Mood and Boost Your Confidence

By

Kelli Stenhouse

Copyright © [2024] Kelli Stenhouse
ISBN: 979-8-9915826-1-2
All rights reserved.

No part of this publication may be used, reproduced, stored in a retrieval system, or transmitted in any form or by any means—such as electronic, photocopying, or recording—without the prior written permission of the copyright owner.

The views expressed in this work are solely those of the author.

Printed in the United States of America.

Dedication

Thank you to my mom for teaching me to be my best, do my best and always look my best while doing it. This book is dedicated to you with all my love and gratitude.

This book is also dedicated to my fellow fashionistas who understand that clothing is not just fabric but a canvas for confidence and a tool for empowerment. May this book inspire you to embrace your unique style, harness the magic of fashion, and uncover the joy of feeling truly confident in your own skin.

This journey is for you—here's to dressing better and feeling better every day!

Introduction

Imagine starting each day with a sense of excitement and self-assurance, knowing that what you wear not only reflects your personality but also enhances your mood and confidence. This book is your guide to achieving just that.

Clothing is more than fabric and design; it's a powerful tool that can influence how we feel about ourselves and how the world perceives us. The right outfit can elevate your spirits, boost your self-esteem, and empower you to take on challenges with a renewed sense of vigor. It can transform a gloomy day into one filled with optimism and possibilities.

In the following pages, you will uncover the powerful link between your wardrobe and your emotional well-being. Together, we will explore how the colors, styles and fits can elevate your mood and empower you to feel your best. By the end, you'll have the tools to build a wardrobe that not only enhances your appearance but also fuels your confidence, making you feel truly unstoppable.

This journey is about more than just fashion; it's about self-discovery and self-expression. You'll learn to understand your unique style, embrace your individuality, and dress in a way that reflects your true self. Whether you're preparing for a big presentation, a casual day out, or a special event, you'll find practical tips and insights to help you make mindful clothing choices that align with your goals and aspirations.

As you turn these pages, you'll begin a path of self-discovery and empowerment, learning how to harness the power of clothing to nurture your mental and emotional well-being. "Dress Better, Feel Better" is more than just a guide to fashion—it is an exploration of how intentional clothing choices can positively impact your emotional health and overall quality of life. By embracing the principles of mindful dressing and understanding the mental effects of fashion, you can harness the power of your wardrobe to enhance your confidence, mood, and self-esteem. This book investigates the psychology of fashion, illustrating how your wardrobe choices are more than just a reflection of your style—they are a vital component of your mental well-being.

Get ready to start a transformative journey. By the end of this book, you'll not only have a deeper understanding of how clothing affects your mood and confidence, but you'll also gain practical tools to create a wardrobe that works for you and possess the skills to dress in a way that empowers you every single day.

As you begin this voyage, you'll learn to make clothing choices that highlight and amplify your best self. Get ready to tap into the potential of your wardrobe and unlock a new level of confidence and well-being. Embrace the principles of mindful dressing and discover how a well-curated wardrobe can lead to a more confident, vibrant, and fulfilled you. Welcome to a new perspective on style and self-care. Let's begin this exciting adventure together!

"You can have anything you want in life if you dress for it."
– Edith Head

TABLE OF CONTENTS

DEDICATION — i

INTRODUCTION — ii

CHAPTER 1 — 01
Dressed for Success: Unlocking the Benefits of Dressing Well

CHAPTER 2 — 09
Polished and Poised: Essential Grooming and Style Basics

CHAPTER 3 — 27
Confidence Unveiled: Beyond the Threads

CHAPTER 4 — 42
Embracing Self-Love, Empowerment, and Your Best Features

CHAPTER 5 — 48
Flattering Fits and Mastering the Art of Dressing for Your Body Type

CHAPTER 6 — 57
Finding Your Personal Style: What's Your Style Profile

CHAPTER 7 — 63
Your Unique Style: Discover Your Signature Look

CHAPTER 8　　　　　　　　　　68
Understanding Color and How It Impacts Mood

CHAPTER 9　　　　　　　　　　74
Color Harmony: Mastering the Art of Outfit Coordination

CHAPTER 10　　　　　　　　　84
Adding a Pop of Color: Simple Tricks to Energize Your Wardrobe

CHAPTER 11　　　　　　　　　87
Tone it Right: Secrets of Skin Undertones

CHAPTER 12　　　　　　　　　94
Outfit Magic: Crafting Your Look in Four Simple Steps

CHAPTER 13　　　　　　　　　100
Accessorize to Mesmerize- Elevating Your Look with the Perfect Details

CHAPTER 14　　　　　　　　　118
Neat Closets, Happy Minds: The Mental Health Benefits of Organization

CHAPTER 15　　　　　　　　　122
Clear the Closet Chaos

TABLE OF CONTENTS

Chapter 01

Dressed for Success

Unlocking the Benefits of Dressing Well

Dressing well is a powerful means of personal empowerment. It goes beyond appearance, touching the core of who we are and how we see ourselves. More than just wearing clothes, it's a profound form of self-expression, a way to share our identity and values with the world. Dressing well is an act of self-respect and a vital investment in our happiness and success. By choosing clothes that make us feel good and reflect our best selves, we not only enhance our appearance but also nurture our inner confidence and self-worth. It's a daily ritual that connects us to our identity, boosts our self-esteem, and helps us navigate the world with grace and assurance. Dressing well is a powerful tool that can enhance your mood and overall mental well-being.

It's a daily opportunity to invest in yourself, boost your confidence, and express your unique personality. Dressing well can notably impact your mood and overall mental well-being. Embrace the transformative power of clothing and let it elevate your life in ways you never imagined!

Let's take a look at 9 simple reasons why you should always try to dress your best:

01) It Enhances Perception

It is a fact that people will consciously and subconsciously judge you based on your outward appearance. Before you even open your mouth to say hello, your outfit and overall appearance have already spoken volumes about you. Although dressing well does not automatically make you a leader, it can impact how others perceive you, your credibility, and your reliability.

Dressing well helps you create a consistent personal image and first impression. You influence other people's reactions to you. So, when you are more deliberate about your clothing, it endorses the image you wish to project.

Studies have shown that better-dressed people are more likely to be given better service, greater employment opportunities, are more successful in attracting potential romantic interests, and receive better treatment than those less mindful of fashion. Your style is the easiest way to tell the world who you are without having to say a word. Therefore, you must invest time and effort to make sure that you always look great. This is because your appearance dramatically influences how others see and treat you.

02 It Makes You Feel Good!

There's a remarkable confidence that comes from knowing you look great. It boosts your self-belief and reassures you of your ability to achieve something extraordinary. Being able to put together a stylish outfit in the morning will definitely boost your confidence and get your day started on a high note. You will walk out of the house feeling like a winner and ready to achieve your goals for the day. Although dressing well does not solve all your problems, it puts you in the right mindset and mood to tackle any challenges that come your way. Also, all the positive interactions and compliments from others will really boost your mood and reinforce your self-esteem!

03 It Is a Form of Self-Care

Dressing well is an integral part of self-care because it makes you look and feel good about yourself. Besides, when something is important to you, you take the time and effort to care for it. By dressing well, you subconsciously remind yourself that you are important, matter, and deserve to be taken care of. Therefore, if you struggle with low self-esteem or always feel like you do not matter, dressing well is a perfect way to remind you that you are more valuable than anything else. Dressing well is a symbolic gesture of self-respect and care. This act of self-respect can improve your mood and reinforce a positive self-image.

04 It Encourages Creativity and Risk-Taking

Creating different outfits can be challenging, especially when your wardrobe is limited! You may have to stretch your creativity and get out of your comfort zone to dress well. Once you learn more about style, your creativity increases, and outfit combinations become easy. In my experience, having a limited budget and fewer options unleashed my creativity—for example, different ways of using accessories (like turning a scarf into a belt).

05 Boosts Confidence

When you dress well, you feel more confident. That confidence radiates from within, affecting how you carry yourself and interact with others. A well-chosen outfit can make you feel empowered, ready to tackle any challenge that comes your way.

06 Elevates Mood

Colors, styles, and textures can influence your emotions. Bright colors can lift your spirits, while comfortable fabrics can provide a sense of coziness and security. Dressing in a way that makes you happy can set a positive tone for the entire day.

07) Enhances Self-Expression

Your clothing is a powerful form of self-expression. It tells the world who you are without saying a word. When you dress in a way that mirrors your true self, you feel more authentic and in harmony with your inner identity.

08) Increases Productivity

When you dress the part, you're more likely to feel motivated and focused. Dressing well can create a psychological shift that primes your mind for productivity, helping you achieve your goals with greater ease and determination.

 Supports Mental Health

Dressing well can be a form of self-therapy. It can provide a sense of control and normalcy, especially during challenging times. When you look good, you feel good, and this can have a profound impact on your mental health.

"Self-care is not a luxury; it's a necessity. Nurture your mind, body, and spirit, and watch your life bloom."
-Unknown

Chapter 02

Polished and Poised

Essential Grooming and Style Basics

In a world where first impressions are crucial, being well-groomed and mastering the basics of style are essential to unlocking a confident, radiant version of yourself. Imagine walking into any room and instantly feeling a surge of self-assurance because you know you look your best. This chapter is your gateway to achieving that feeling every day.

Grooming and basic style are not just about adhering to social norms or following trends. They are about self-respect, self-expression, and setting the stage for the best version of you to shine through. When you take the time to groom yourself well and understand the basics of style, you send a powerful message to the world: you are ready to embrace opportunities, face challenges, and make meaningful connections.

In the following pages, we will explore the foundational elements of grooming and style that every person should know. This chapter covers everything from skincare routines that leave you glowing to understanding how to choose clothing that complements your body type. You'll discover simple yet effective tips for maintaining a neat appearance and learn the art of selecting timeless pieces that form the cornerstone of a versatile wardrobe.

But beyond the practical advice, this chapter is about transformation. It's about recognizing that taking care of your appearance is an act of self-love. It's about realizing that when you feel good about your appearance, you project a positive energy that can influence every aspect of your life. Whether you're preparing for an important meeting, a casual day out, or a special event, being polished and poised sets the tone for success.

Let this chapter be your guide to mastering the essentials of grooming and style. Embrace these practices not as chores but as rituals that celebrate your unique identity and enhance your confidence. As you read on, you'll find that the journey to looking polished and poised is not just about changing your appearance; it's about transforming how you feel about yourself.

It's time to understand the power of being well-groomed and stylish and to step into a world where you can always feel polished and poised.

Examples of Well-Groomed

Clean and Styled Hair

Hair should be clean, neatly styled, and appropriate for the occasion. This includes regular trims to avoid split ends and maintaining a hairstyle that suits your face shape and personal style.

Fresh Breath and Oral Hygiene

Regular brushing, flossing, and dental check-ups ensure fresh breath and a healthy smile. Using mouthwash and breath mints as needed, especially before social or professional interactions.

Clear Skin

Maintaining a skincare routine that keeps your skin clean, moisturized, and protected from the sun. This includes addressing any skin concerns, such as acne or dryness, with appropriate treatments.

Manicured Nails

Keeping nails trimmed, clean, and filed. This includes both fingernails and toenails. They should be free from dirt and hangnails. For those who prefer nail polish, make sure it is neatly applied and not chipped.

Well-Fitting Clothes

Your clothes should fit well and be appropriate for your body type. This includes tailoring garments if necessary to ensure they are neither too tight nor too loose.

Clean and Pressed Clothes

Wearing clothes that are clean, free from stains, and neatly pressed is critical. Any spots or spills should be promptly treated.

Polished Shoes	**Tidy Facial Hair**
Always shoes that are clean, polished, and in good condition. This includes ensuring that laces are tied properly and that any scuffs or scratches are addressed. To deodorize shoes, you can sprinkle the inside with baking soda. Regularly clean shoes with a damp cloth, leather cleaner or magic eraser to keep them looking fresh.	For men, maintaining well-groomed facial hair, whether it's a clean shave or a neatly trimmed beard or mustache, is key. For women, managing unwanted facial hair and keeping eyebrows well-shaped are essential steps.
Appropriate Accessories	**Subtle and Pleasant Fragrance**
Choose accessories that complement your outfit and are in good condition. This includes clean and polished jewelry, belts, bags, and watches that add to your overall look.	Use a pleasant but subtle fragrance, such as cologne or perfume, without overdoing it. This also includes using deodorant to stay fresh throughout the day.
Proper Posture and Body Language	**Personal Hygiene**
Make an effort to maintain good posture and display confident body language, which enhances your overall appearance and demeanor.	Regular bathing, using body lotion, and ensuring your body is clean and well cared for is essential. This also includes using products that suit your skin type and personal needs.

By incorporating these practices into your daily routine, you can present yourself as well-groomed, polished, and poised, ready to make a positive impression in any situation.

Examples of Sloppy and Frumpy

Wrinkled Clothing

Wearing shirts, pants, or dresses that are visibly wrinkled gives the impression of neglect and lack of care for one's appearance.

Stains and Spills

Clothes with noticeable stains, spills, or food marks can make you appear unkempt and inattentive to personal hygiene.

Ill-Fitting Clothes

Wearing clothes that are too baggy, too tight, or mismatched in size can create a sloppy look. This includes pants that sag or drag on the ground and shirts that are too loose or cling in the wrong places.

Unkempt Hair

Hair that is greasy, messy, or unbrushed contributes to a frumpy appearance. Split ends, overgrown roots, or hair that looks unwashed can diminish the effort put into the rest of your look.

Untidy Shoes

Shoes that are scuffed, dirty, or inappropriate for the outfit can distract from an otherwise decent ensemble. For instance, wearing worn-out sneakers with formal attire can make you look disheveled.

Overly Casual Attire

Wearing overly casual clothes, like sweatpants, pajama bottoms, or old T-shirts, in settings that require more polished attire can come off as frumpy. This is especially true in professional or social environments where a more put-together appearance is expected.

Mismatched or Outdated Clothing	**Poorly Maintained Accessories**
Wearing outdated styles or mismatched pieces can make you look frumpy. This includes patterns that clash or wearing clothes that are visibly out of style.	Accessories that are broken, frayed, or otherwise poorly maintained, such as belts with worn-out holes, bags with tears, or tarnished jewelry, can contribute to a sloppy look.
Lack of Personal Hygiene	**Overly Layered or Bulky Clothing**
Neglecting basic grooming practices, such as not shaving, not trimming nails, or not using deodorant, can make you appear sloppy and unkempt.	Wearing too many layers or overly bulky clothes can make you look frumpy, especially if the layers don't complement each other or create a streamlined silhouette.
Tattered or Worn-Out Clothes	**Visible Undergarments**
Clothes with frayed hems, holes, or visible signs of wear and tear can make you appear disheveled and inattentive to your appearance.	Allowing undergarments to be visible, whether bra straps are showing or pants are exposing underwear, can look sloppy and inappropriate in most settings.

Avoiding a sloppy and frumpy appearance is vital for several reasons that extend beyond merely looking good. Here are 6 compelling reasons to strive for a polished and put-together look:

MENTAL WELL-BEING

There is a strong connection between grooming and mental health. Engaging in regular grooming routines can provide a sense of normalcy and control, reduce stress, and contribute to an overall sense of well-being and happiness.

RESPECT FOR YOURSELF AND OTHERS

Taking care of your appearance shows that you value yourself and respect those around you. It reflects a level of self-discipline and self-respect that can be inspiring to others.

PROFESSIONALISM

In many professional settings, maintaining a polished appearance is essential. It demonstrates respect for your role and your workplace, and it can influence how colleagues, clients, and superiors perceive your competence and reliability.

FIRST IMPRESSIONS MATTER

The way you present yourself significantly influences how others perceive you. A neat and well-groomed appearance can create a positive first impression, while a sloppy look can lead to negative judgments about your professionalism and attention to detail.

ENHANCED SOCIAL INTERACTIONS

People are generally more inclined to engage with and trust those who present themselves well. A neat appearance can facilitate better social interactions and relationships, both personally and professionally.

ATTENTION TO DETAIL

A well-maintained appearance indicates that you pay attention to details. This trait is often associated with thoroughness and conscientiousness in other areas of life and work.

Being well-groomed goes beyond just looking neat; it involves a holistic approach to personal care that affects how you feel and how others perceive you. Here's a comprehensive guide to achieving and maintaining impeccable grooming habits:

Hair Care

Hair Cuts: Keep your hair looking its best with regular trims every 6-8 weeks to maintain shape and health.

Choose a Style that Suits You: Select a hairstyle that complements your face shape and personal style.

Washing: Wash your hair as needed based on your hair type and lifestyle. For most people, 2-3 times a week is sufficient.

Conditioning: Use a conditioner that suits your hair type to keep it hydrated and manageable.

Styling: Use appropriate styling products and tools to achieve a look that enhances your features. Avoid excessive heat or harsh products.

Scalp Care: Occasionally exfoliate your scalp to remove buildup and promote healthy hair growth. Ensure your scalp is well-moisturized, especially if you have dry skin.

Skin Care

Cleansing: Cleanse your face twice a day with a gentle cleanser suited to your skin type to remove dirt, oil, and impurities.

Exfoliation: Exfoliate 1-2 times a week to remove dead skin cells and improve skin texture.

Hydration: Use a moisturizer daily to keep your skin hydrated and supple. Choose a product that matches your skin type (e.g., oily, dry, combination).

Sun Protection: Apply sunscreen with at least SPF 30 daily, even on cloudy days, to protect your skin from UV damage and prevent premature aging.

Treatments: Address specific skin concerns (acne, hyperpigmentation) with targeted treatments or products.

Regular Check-ups: Consider periodic facials or professional skin treatments as needed.

Facial Hair

Shaving and Regular Trimming: Keep facial hair trimmed to a manageable length. Invest in a good razor and shaving cream to prevent irritation.

Proper Technique: Shave in the direction of hair growth to avoid ingrown hairs and razor burns.

Beard Care: If you have a beard, trim and shape it regularly to maintain a neat appearance.

Conditioning: Use beard oil or balm to keep facial hair soft and the skin beneath it hydrated.

Nail Care

Manicures: Keep fingernails trimmed and filed to avoid snags and breakage. Remove any dirt or debris from under the nails.

Pedicures: Keep toenails trimmed and filed to avoid snags and breakage. Remove any dirt or debris from under the nails.

Cuticle Care: Gently push back cuticles and avoid cutting them to prevent infection.

Polishing and Healthy Nails: Use nail polish occasionally and ensure that it is removed properly to avoid staining. Consider giving your nails a break from polish to prevent damage.

Oral Hygiene

Brushing: Brush your teeth at least twice a day with fluoride toothpaste to prevent cavities and maintain fresh breath.

Technique: Use a soft-bristled toothbrush and brush for at least 2 minutes.

Flossing: Floss daily to remove food particles and plaque between teeth to prevent gum disease and cavities.

Dentist Visits: Schedule regular dental check-ups and cleanings every 6 months.

Body Care

Bathing: Bathe or shower daily to keep your body clean. Use a gentle body wash or soap suited to your skin type.

Exfoliation: Use a body scrub or exfoliating glove once or twice a week to remove dead skin cells.

Deodorant: Apply deodorant or antiperspirant daily to stay fresh and odor-free.

Moisturizing: Apply body lotion after showering to keep your skin hydrated and smooth.

Clothing and Personal Style

Maintenance: Ensure your clothes are clean, pressed, and in good condition. Avoid wearing items that are stained or excessively wrinkled.

Proper Fit: Wear clothing that fits well and complements your body shape. Ill-fitting clothes can affect your overall appearance and comfort.

Accessories: Choose accessories that enhance your outfit and add a touch of personal style.

Overall Hygiene

Hand Hygiene: Wash your hands regularly with soap and water, especially before eating or touching your face.

Foot Care: Keep your feet clean and dry. Use foot powder if necessary to prevent odor.

Regular Checks: Pay attention to areas that might need extra care, such as behind the ears and between the toes.

Being well-groomed goes beyond just looking neat; it's a reflection of self-respect and personal pride. It's about presenting yourself in a way that conveys confidence, attention to detail, and a deep understanding of your own worth. Good grooming involves more than maintaining a clean appearance; it's about cultivating a sense of inner harmony that radiates outward.

When you are well-groomed, you're not just adhering to societal standards of cleanliness and order—you're embracing the power of self-care. Each carefully chosen detail, from the perfect hairstyle to well-fitted clothes, contributes to a polished image that enhances your overall presence. This meticulous attention to grooming signals that you value yourself and your role in the world.

More than just aesthetics, quality grooming can profoundly impact how you feel about yourself. It boosts your confidence, making you feel more capable and ready to face any challenge. It helps you project a professional image, creating a positive impression in both personal and professional settings.

Ultimately, being well-groomed is about creating a consistent and positive image that reflects your best self. It's a commitment to excellence in how you present yourself to the world, and it's a powerful tool for building self-esteem and achieving personal and professional success. Remember, grooming is an ongoing process and should be adjusted based on your personal needs and lifestyle. Maintaining impeccable grooming habits is a powerful form of self-expression and self-respect. It's about taking control of how you present yourself to the world and embracing the confidence and positivity that come with knowing you are putting your best foot forward every day.

> **"Style is a way to say who you are without having to speak."**
> – *Rachel Zoe*

Chapter 03

Confidence Unveiled

Beyond the Threads

True confidence extends well beyond the clothes we wear. While clothing can undoubtedly enhance our appearance, the core of confidence lies in our inner beliefs and self-perception.

Imagine stepping into a room with an aura of self-assurance, not because of the designer label on your jacket, but because you genuinely believe in your own worth and abilities. This chapter is about unlocking that inner confidence that transforms not only how you present yourself but also how you interact with the world.

Genuine confidence stems from self-awareness, self-acceptance, and a positive mindset. It's about understanding that while your wardrobe can complement your confidence, it is your inner strength and self-belief that truly define it. You must learn to build and maintain this inner confidence, so that you can shine from within regardless of what you're wearing.

From cultivating a positive self-image to developing resilience and assertiveness, this chapter will provide you with tools and insights to fortify your self-confidence. You'll learn tips to harness your unique strengths, embrace your individuality, and project a sense of confidence that resonates deeply with others.

Personal style is more than following fashion trends; it's a powerful tool for self-expression and a reflection of our unique identities. It empowers individuals by boosting confidence, fostering authenticity, and unleashing true potential.

Showing authenticity and self-expression involves embracing and projecting your true self in a way that feels genuine and meaningful to you. Here are ways you can achieve this:

Understand Yourself

Self-Reflection: Take time to reflect on your values, passions, and what truly matters to you. Knowing yourself deeply is the foundation of authenticity.

Embrace Strengths and Weaknesses: Recognize and accept your strengths and areas for growth. Authenticity involves being comfortable with who you are, including your imperfections.

Be True to Your Values

Align Actions with Beliefs: Make decisions and act in ways that are consistent with your core values and beliefs. This alignment helps you stay true to yourself.

Stand Up for What You Believe: Don't shy away from expressing your opinions and standing up for your beliefs, even if they differ from the norm.

Express Your Unique Style

Personalize Your Wardrobe: Choose clothing, accessories, and styles that reflect your personality and preferences. Your fashion choices should feel like an extension of who you are.

Experiment and Evolve: Allow your style to evolve as you do. Experiment with new looks and trends that resonate with you and reflect your current self.

Communicate Openly and Honestly

Be Transparent: Share your thoughts and feelings openly with others. Honest communication fosters genuine connections and allows you to be seen for who you truly are.

Listen Actively: Authenticity is a two-way street. Engage in active listening and show genuine interest in others' perspectives and experiences.

Embrace Your Individuality

Celebrate Uniqueness: Embrace what makes you different. Whether it's a unique skill, perspective, or personal story, celebrating your individuality enriches your self-expression.

Avoid Comparisons: Focus on your own journey rather than comparing yourself to others. Authenticity thrives when you appreciate and honor your unique path.

Be Consistent

Maintain Integrity: Stay true to your principles and character in all situations. Authenticity is about being consistent in your actions and beliefs, regardless of external circumstances.

Follow Through: Keep your commitments and follow through on promises. Reliability and integrity enhance your sense of authenticity.

Practice Self-Acceptance

Acknowledge Your Imperfections: Accept that nobody is perfect and that imperfections are part of what makes you uniquely you.

Cultivate Self-Compassion: Be kind to yourself and practice self-compassion. Treat yourself with the same understanding and care that you would offer a friend.

Engage in Meaningful Activities

Pursue Passions: Engage in activities and hobbies that genuinely interest and excite you. Doing what you love reinforces your sense of self and enhances your authenticity.

Build Genuine Connections: Surround yourself with people who appreciate and support your true self. Authentic relationships are built on mutual respect and understanding.

Reflect and Adjust

Regular Check-Ins: Periodically assess whether your actions and expressions align with your true self. Adjust as needed to stay in tune with who you are.

Seek Feedback: Constructive feedback from trusted friends or mentors can provide insights into how well you're expressing your authentic self.

Showing authenticity and self-expression is about being true to yourself and allowing your genuine personality to shine through in everything you do. It's a continuous journey of self-discovery, acceptance, and growth, and it leads to more meaningful connections and a greater sense of fulfillment.

Personal style allows us to authentically express our inner selves to the world. By aligning our outfits with our values and personality, we enhance self-awareness and embrace our unique qualities without fear of judgment.

Body Positivity and Acceptance

Developing body positivity and acceptance involves cultivating a healthy and loving relationship with your body, recognizing its value beyond appearance, and challenging societal standards. If you are not sure how to do this, here are a few easy ways to help you foster body positivity and acceptance:

Practice Self-Compassion

Be Kind to Yourself: Speak to yourself with kindness and avoid self-critical thoughts. Treat yourself as you would treat a friend.

Acknowledge Imperfections: Understand that imperfections are a natural part of being human. Embrace them as part of your unique self.

Challenge Negative Thoughts

Identify and Reframe: Notice negative self-talk and challenge it. Reframe negative thoughts into positive or neutral ones that reflect your true worth.

Focus on Strengths: Emphasize the positive aspects of your body, such as its strength, abilities, and the things it allows you to do.

Celebrate Your Body

Appreciate Functionality: Recognize and appreciate what your body can do, such as walking, dancing, or hugging loved ones.

Celebrate Achievements: Celebrate your body's achievements and milestones, from fitness goals to personal accomplishments.

Surround Yourself with Positivity

Positive Influences: Follow social media accounts, read books, or engage with communities that promote body positivity and diverse representations of beauty.

Supportive Relationships: Surround yourself with people who support and uplift you and encourage body positivity and self-acceptance.

Avoid Comparisons

Limit Social Media: Be mindful of how social media affects your self-perception. Limit exposure to content that promotes unrealistic beauty standards.

Focus on Yourself: Avoid comparing your body to others. Everyone's body is unique, and comparisons can undermine your sense of self-worth.

Practice Mindful Eating and Movement

Enjoy Food: Develop a healthy relationship with food by focusing on nourishment and enjoyment rather than restriction or guilt.

Move for Joy: Engage in physical activities that you enjoy and that make you feel good rather than focusing solely on appearance-based goals.

Wear What Makes You Feel Good

Comfort and Style: Choose clothing that makes you feel comfortable and confident. Wear what you love, regardless of trends or societal expectations.

Body Acceptance: Select outfits that reflect your personal style and celebrate your body as it is.

Educate Yourself

Learn About Body Positivity: Educate yourself about body positivity and the impact of societal beauty standards. Understanding the broader context can help you challenge these standards.

Seek Inspiration: Read books, listen to podcasts, and engage with content that promotes body acceptance and self-love.

Engage in Positive Self-Care

Pamper Yourself: Engage in self-care practices that make you feel good, whether it's a relaxing bath, a massage, or a favorite hobby.

Prioritize Well-Being: Focus on activities that enhance your overall well-being, such as mindfulness, relaxation, and mental health support.

Seek Professional Support

Therapy and Counseling: If body image issues are affecting your mental health, consider speaking with a therapist or counselor who specializes in body image and self-esteem.

Support Groups: Join support groups or communities focused on body positivity and self-acceptance for shared experiences and encouragement.

Set Realistic Goals

Healthy Goals: Set goals that are centered around health and well-being rather than appearance. Focus on feeling good and being healthy, not just meeting external standards.

Practice Gratitude

Daily Reflection: Take time each day to express gratitude for your body and its capabilities. Acknowledge what you appreciate about yourself and your physical health.

Developing body positivity and acceptance is a continuous expedition that involves shifting your mindset and challenging societal norms. By embracing self-compassion, celebrating your body, and surrounding yourself with positivity, you can build a healthier and more loving relationship with yourself. Creating a personal style that celebrates and embraces our bodies is an empowering journey. By highlighting our favorite features and embracing perceived imperfections, we foster body positivity and redefine beauty standards. Through individual style, we redefine beauty standards by embracing our diverse body shapes and sizes.

Confidence and Self-Esteem

Gaining confidence and self-esteem is a journey of self-discovery and personal growth. It involves building a positive self-image, developing skills, and fostering a healthy mindset. The way we dress has a profound impact on our confidence and self-esteem. When we wear an outfit that makes us feel comfortable, stylish, and true to ourselves, it increases our confidence levels.

When we dress comfortably and stylishly, it boosts our self-esteem, empowering us to navigate social interactions and pursue our goals confidently.

Emotional Well-being and Empowerment

The relationship between personal style and self-empowerment is undeniable. Personal style influences emotional well-being by resonating with our mood. Choosing colors and styles that align with our emotions enhances our energy and resilience, contributing to a sense of empowerment.

Through our personal style, we connect with our authentic selves, cultivate body positivity, and elevate our confidence. Style becomes a catalyst for self-expression and emotional well-being. Let your personal style be a source of empowerment, helping you unlock your true potential and embrace the remarkable journey of self-discovery. Dress not just for fashion, but for empowerment.

Reflect, Reveal, Renew

List and reflect on any negative self-talk or body criticisms you frequently encounter. How can you reframe these thoughts into positive affirmations that reinforce your body confidence?

_____
_____
_____
_____
_____
_____
_____
_____
_____
_____
_____
_____
_____
_____
_____
_____
_____
_____
_____
_____
_____

Reflect on a time when you felt particularly confident and self-assured. What factors or circumstances contributed to that feeling, and how can you recreate or build upon those factors in your daily life?

_____
_____
_____
_____
_____
_____
_____
_____
_____
_____
_____
_____
_____
_____
_____
_____
_____
_____
_____
_____
_____
_____
_____
_____
_____
_____

Think about a time when you felt most confident and comfortable in your clothing. What elements of that outfit made you feel this way.

_____
_____
_____
_____
_____
_____
_____
_____
_____
_____
_____
_____
_____
_____
_____
_____
_____
_____
_____

> "Owning our story and loving ourselves through that process is the bravest thing that we'll ever do."
> - Brene' Brown

Chapter 04

Embracing Self-Love, Empowerment, and Your Best Features

Self-love and empowerment go beyond just recognizing your best features; it's about embracing them with confidence and celebrating the unique beauty that's inherently yours. True confidence shines from within and is closely tied to how you perceive and value yourself. By nurturing self-love and empowering yourself, you elevate your self-esteem and unlock the ability to showcase your best features in a way that feels authentic and uplifting.

Self-love is the foundation of confidence and empowering yourself will lead to a more fulfilling and authentic expression of your beauty. Identify and accentuate your best features, not through external validation, but through a deep-seated appreciation of your individuality. Embracing self-love allows you to present yourself in the most genuine and powerful way possible. As you learn to celebrate your unique features and embrace self-love, you'll find that confidence naturally follows.

Embracing your best features is a celebration of your unique beauty and individuality. It's about recognizing and highlighting the attributes that make you stand out, not for validation, but as a genuine reflection of who you are. When you embrace your best features, you're not just enhancing your appearance but acknowledging and celebrating your inherent worth.

Imagine looking in the mirror and seeing not just a reflection but a canvas of your personal strengths and attributes. It's about seeing beyond societal standards and trends and instead focusing on what makes you uniquely beautiful. Whether it's your radiant smile, expressive eyes, or how your laughter lights up a room, these features are a testament to your individuality.

Embracing your best features starts with self-love. It requires a shift from comparing yourself to others to appreciating your own uniqueness. When you focus on your standout qualities, you build a foundation of confidence that shines from within. This confidence is magnetic; it draws others to you and empowers you to face the world with authenticity and grace.

Discover and celebrate what you love about yourself! Recognize how these features contribute to your identity and express them with pride. It's not about perfection but about acknowledging your personal beauty and letting it shine. When you embrace your best features, you give yourself permission to be fully and unapologetically yourself.

By highlighting what you cherish most about yourself, you set the stage for others to see you as you see yourself —confident, beautiful, and empowered. Embrace your best features as physical attributes and expressions of your inner strength and unique spirit. In doing so, you create a life where you are celebrated for who you indeed are, and you inspire others to do the same. If you struggle in this area and you're not quite sure where to start, try this:

Shift Your Mindset

Celebrate Your Body: Focus on what you love about your body rather than perceived flaws. Each body is unique and beautiful in its own way.

Reject Unrealistic Standards: Recognize that media portrayals of "ideal" bodies are often unrealistic and unattainable. Embrace the diversity of natural bodies.

Positive Affirmations: Practice affirmations that reinforce self-love and acceptance. Remind yourself daily of your worth beyond physical appearance.

Learn Your Body Shape and Style

Know Your Proportions: Understanding your body shape helps you choose clothes that flatter your figure. Whether you're pear-shaped, apple-shaped, hourglass, or any other shape, there are styles that will enhance your natural silhouette.

Experiment with Fashion: Try different styles and silhouettes to discover what makes you feel confident and comfortable. Don't be afraid to step out of your comfort zone and explore new trends.

Choose Clothes Wisely

Focus on Fit: Well-fitting clothing is vital for feeling confident. Tailor clothes if needed to ensure they enhance your shape and proportions. It's okay to go up a size as needed. No one is looking at (or cares about) the tag inside your clothes. Wear clothes that fit as it will improve your confidence. Being comfortable is essential.

Highlight Your Assets: Accentuate parts of your body that you love. For example, if you love your legs, opt for skirts or dresses that show them off.

Colors and Patterns: Play with colors and patterns that you enjoy. Dark colors can be slimming, while bold patterns can add personality to your outfit.

Accessorize Thoughtfully

Statement Pieces: Use accessories like jewelry, scarves, or belts to draw attention to areas you want to highlight or add a pop of interest to your outfit.

Shoes: Choose shoes that not only complement your outfit but also make you feel confident and comfortable.

Confidence in Action

Body Language: Stand tall with good posture. Confidence is as much about how you carry yourself as it is about what you wear.

Practice Self-Care: Take care of your body and mind through healthy habits, exercise, and activities that make you feel good.

Community and Support

Find Like-Minded Individuals: Surround yourself with supportive friends, family, or online communities that promote body positivity and self-acceptance.

Share Your Journey: Inspire others by sharing your journey towards self-acceptance and body positivity. Your story can encourage others to embrace their uniqueness.

Remember, that accepting your body and dressing confidently regardless of size or shape is all about self-love, empowerment, and understanding how to accentuate your best features. Confidence comes from within. When you embrace and celebrate your body, dressing confidently becomes a natural extension of your self-love and acceptance.

"Body positivity is not about body size; it's about loving and accepting yourself as you are. You are not a size. You are not a number. You are a beautiful, unique individual."
— Unknown

Chapter 05

Flattering Fits and Mastering the Art of Dressing for Your Body Type

Choosing clothing styles and silhouettes that flatter your unique body shape can significantly elevate your appearance and boost your confidence. The key to dressing well lies in discovering how to enhance your natural shape, allowing you to feel both confident and stylish. Understanding your body type and selecting clothing that complements it isn't about conforming to a standard—it's about embracing and celebrating your distinct physique.

Every body type has its own set of characteristics and features, and the key to looking your best lies in recognizing these and selecting outfits that highlight your best attributes. When you dress in a way that aligns with your body type, you create a harmonious look that enhances your overall appearance and ultimately boosts your confidence.

We'll delve into different body types and offer practical tips for choosing clothing that enhances each one. From mastering the principles of proportion and fit to selecting the suitable fabrics and styles, this chapter will guide you in creating a wardrobe that showcases your personal style while highlighting your natural beauty.

Prepare to discover how the right clothing can transform your look and make you feel great in your own skin. By mastering the art of dressing for your body type, you'll not only enhance your physical appearance but also build a wardrobe that empowers you to express yourself with confidence and flair.

The hourglass shape is characterized by balanced proportions with a well-defined waist, creating a silhouette that resembles an hourglass.

Key Features: Look for a defined waistline when viewed from the front. Bust and hips measurements are within a few inches of each other. Balanced appearance with curves at the bust and hips.

Flattering Styles

- Fitted Dresses and Tops: Highlight your waistline.
- Wrap Dresses: Emphasize your waist and curves.
- High-Waisted Bottoms: Accentuate your waist.
- V-necklines and Scoop Necks: Flatter your bust.

The apple shape is characterized by a fuller upper body and a less defined waist.

Key Features: Waist measurement is similar or more prominent than bust measurement. A waistline that is less defined than other body shapes. Weight tends to accumulate around the abdomen. Fuller midsection with a less defined waist. Bust is usually larger.

Flattering Styles

- Empire Waist Dresses: Define just below the bust.
- Blouses, Tunics and Flowy Tops: Skim over the midsection.
- V-necklines: Draw attention upwards.
- A-line Dresses and Skirts: Create balance and shape.

The pear shape is characterized by a lower body that is fuller compared to the upper body.

Key Features: Hips are noticeably wider than shoulders. Defined waistline when viewed from the side. Weight tends to be carried in the lower body. Narrower shoulders and waist with fuller hips and thighs.

Flattering Styles:

- Dark-colored Bottoms: Minimize hips.
- Structured Jackets and Tops: Broaden shoulders.
- Fit-and-flare Dresses: Highlight the waist while balancing the hips.
- Wide-leg Pants: Create balance with the lower body.

The rectangle shape, also known as the straight or athletic shape, is characterized by a more uniform proportion across the body.

Key Features: Shoulder, bust, and hip measurements are similar. Waist is not significantly narrower than the bust or hips. Generally straighter appearance from shoulders to hips. Straight and balanced from shoulders to hips.

Flattering Styles

- Belts and Waist Details: Creates definition at the waist and the illusion of curves.
- Peplum Tops and Dresses: Adds volume to the waist and the illusion of curves.
- Layered Tops: Add dimension.
- Tailored Jackets and Blazers: Create the illusion of curves. Define the waistline.

The inverted triangle shape, also known as the apple or broad-shouldered shape, is characterized by a wider upper body compared to the lower body.

Key Features: Broad shoulders and narrower hips. Shoulders are noticeably wider than hips. Bust measurement may be larger than hip measurement. Waist may not be as defined as in other shapes.

Flattering Styles

- V-necklines: Create balance with shoulders.
- Flared Skirts and Pants: Add volume to lower body.
- Wrap Dresses: Define waist and soften shoulders.
- Bootcut or Flared Jeans: Balance proportions.
- A-line Skirts: Create volume at the hips.
- Structured Jackets with defined waist: Balance the upper body.

General Tips for All Body Shapes

Proportion: Balance fitted pieces with looser ones for a streamlined look.

Fabric: Choose fabrics that drape well and provide structure where needed.

Tailoring: Invest in alterations to ensure clothing fits your body perfectly.

Accessories: Use accessories strategically to draw attention to areas you want to highlight.

Understanding Your Body Shape

- Stand in front of a mirror and observe your proportions.
- Note where your body naturally curves in or out.
- Pay attention to where your body widens or narrows.
- Understanding your body shape helps you choose clothing that flatters your figure by emphasizing your best features and balancing proportions.
- It's important to remember that everyone's body is unique, and these shapes are just general guidelines to help you navigate fashion choices effectively.

Remember that we are all shaped differently (and beautifully)! Maybe you're a blend of two or more body types. By understanding your body shape and choosing styles that accentuate your best features while minimizing areas of concern, you can create a wardrobe that enhances your confidence and personal style.

These three basic ideas below will help you dress any body shape:

Draw attention to your best body features

For a flawless look, concentrate on your strong points. Perhaps do a sleeveless look to flaunt your gorgeous arms or miniskirts for striking legs. Also, use lines to look leaner or taller or highlight your curves. For instance, parallel lines could make you appear plumper, and perpendicular ones can make you look thinner. In contrast, stripes/pinstripes can make you appear taller or elongate your torso—moreover, fitting clothes, polos, or V-neck tones down a bulging torso or chest.

Balance

Wear outfits complimenting your bone structure while balancing your bust, waist, hips, and shoulders. Wear padded coats to make the shoulders seem bigger. To enhance a rectangular shape, focus on broadening the shoulder line while creating a leaner appearance for the lower body. For an oval or round shape, aim to downplay the midsection. If you have small hips, opt for figure-hugging bottoms. Steer clear of baggy clothes, as they tend to conceal your natural shape.

Consider colors

Flower-patterned clothes and those with light/bright hues are more enticing than dull or gloomy colors. A dark pair of jeans, a skirt, or a dress can make you look slimmer. Patterns and bold colors can widen the hips or bust. Use these tips to blur or accentuate what you want. In this chapter, we explored the essential basics of dressing for your body type, equipping you with the knowledge and tools to enhance your natural shape and boost your confidence. Understanding and embracing your body type is the first step towards creating a wardrobe that not only fits well but also flatters and celebrates your unique figure. By recognizing and honoring your individual body shape, you will embark on a journey of self-discovery and self-love.

Hopefully, this chapter:

- Provided you with the guidance needed to transform your wardrobe into a collection that reflects your inner beauty and strength.
- Empowered you to make fashion choices that align with your true self.
- Inspired you to step out confidently, knowing that you look and feel your best.

As you continue this journey, remember that your wardrobe is a powerful tool for self-expression and self-love. Celebrate your unique figure, embrace your individuality, and let your style reflect the incredible person you are. With this knowledge, you are now ready to face the world with renewed confidence and joy, knowing that you have mastered the art of dressing for your body type. Remember, we are all beautiful and deserving of stylish, well-fitting clothes that highlight our best features.

"The way you see yourself is how the world will see you."
– Unknown

Chapter 06

Finding Your Personal Style

What's Your Style Profile

Personal Style- it's what turns heads and gets you noticed. It is a form of self-expression, but also a means of communication. How you dress tells people who you really are! Defining your own style type gives you a place to begin. It's a way to uncover and come to grips with who you are and to determine what is appropriate for your personal style.

Your personality is often a strong indicator of what type of style suits you best. Select the line with the words that best describe your personality:

- ☐ Well-groomed, sophisticated, organized
- ☐ Trendsetter, label-aware, spontaneous
- ☐ Direct, confident, independent
- ☐ Friendly, casual, sporty, and athletic
- ☐ Romantic, empathetic, sensitive
- ☐ Bold, open-minded, enjoys life to the fullest
- ☐ Creative, artsy, laid-back, unconventional
- ☐ Futuristic, adventurous, cultural, and musical

Imagine you won a gift card to buy a new outfit. What line best describes the outfit you would choose:

- ☐ Slacks, long cardigan with a matching skinny belt, and a pair of ankle boots
- ☐ Trendy fashion leggings, latest tunic top or dress, chunky gladiator heels
- ☐ Fitted dress, statement necklace, cuff bracelet, and a pair of heels

- ☐ Jeans, simple tunic top or T-shirt, sneakers, and small stud earrings
- ☐ Long floral print dress with ruffles, pearl drop earrings, charm bracelet, and a pair of sequined sandals
- ☐ Print dress, bold with eye-popping jacket, and multi-colored jewelry
- ☐ Anything with bright, ethnic patterns, slouchy boots, and exotic jewelry
- ☐ Cropped leather jacket, black skinny jeans, bold and bright colored top, and studded shoes

You're in a shoe store. What type of shoes do you instinctively look for?

- ☐ Simple ballerina flats or loafers
- ☐ Anything that's shown under 'Newest Arrivals'
- ☐ High-heel pumps
- ☐ A pair of simple canvas sneakers like Vans or Converse

- ☐ Espadrilles, wedges, or anything with florals or lace
- ☐ Moccasins, boots, or booties
- ☐ Designer sneakers (e.g., Nike, Adidas, Christian Dior, Gucci, etc.)

If you were to win a closet makeover from your favorite stores, which would that be?

- ☐ Banana Republic, Gap, Old Navy, J. Crew
- ☐ Ann Taylor, Macy's, Chicos
- ☐ Kohls, H&M, Target
- ☐ TJ Maxx, Marshalls, Ross
- ☐ Urban Outfitters, Free People, vintage, consignment, and thrift stores
- ☐ Other

What types of accessories dominate your wardrobe?

- ☐ Pearls, simple chain jewelry, dainty and nostalgic jewelry
- ☐ The latest fashionable shoes
- ☐ Cuff bracelets and other bold, statement jewelry
- ☐ Belts, watches, and hats
- ☐ Exotic print scarves, cool hats, wood and shell jewelry
- ☐ Large hoop earrings, studded jewelry, cool sunglasses
- ☐ Designer bags

How would you best define your personal tastes in clothes and style?

- ☐ Classic
- ☐ Preppy
- ☐ Bohemian (Boho) chic
- ☐ Trendy and edgy

- ☐ Modern
- ☐ Feminine and ladylike
- ☐ Not sure

Where do you turn for style inspiration?

- ☐ Pinterest
- ☐ Friends and family
- ☐ Street style
- ☐ Celebrities
- ☐ People at work
- ☐ Magazines
- ☐ Other

"Fashion is the science of appearances, and it inspires one to believe in oneself."
– Alexander McQueen

Chapter 07

Your Unique Style

Discover Your Signature Look

Take a moment to respond to the prompts below. This exercise will help you articulate your style preferences more clearly and confidently. Exploring these aspects can lead to a better understanding of personal style, allowing for a wardrobe that reflects individuality and enhances self-expression.

Describe what you are usually wearing when you feel most confident.

_____
_____
_____
_____

Is there anything you would like to change about your style?

_____
_____
_____
_____

What are your favorite pieces of clothing in your closet right now? Why are they your favorite?

_____
_____
_____
_____

Are there particular fabrics or textures that you find most comfortable or appealing?

_____
_____
_____
_____

What are you wearing when you receive compliments from others?

_____
_____
_____
_____

What do you want your personal style and wardrobe to say about you?

_____
_____
_____
_____

What colors do you find yourself gravitating towards in your wardrobe?

_____
_____
_____
_____

Are there specific colors that make you feel confident or express your mood?

_____
_____
_____
_____

How does your daily routine and lifestyle influence your clothing choices?

_____
_____
_____
_____

Do you prefer form-fitting clothes that highlight your figure or looser styles that provide freedom of movement?

_____
_____
_____
_____

Do you prefer versatile pieces that can be styled in different ways, or statement pieces that make a bold impression?

_____
_____
_____
_____

"Color is a power which directly influences the soul."
– Wassily Kandinsky

Chapter 08

Understanding Color and How It Impacts Mood

Color psychology is a fascinating yet often overlooked field that examines how we respond to different colors. While scientific research on this topic may be limited, it's evident that colors can impact our decisions in various ways. Many industries use this understanding to influence our choices.

There's a reason why we describe certain emotions in a specific way — seeing red, feeling blue, being green with envy — color and mood are directly connected. Color is a powerful communication tool and can be used to signal action, influence mood, and drive physiological reactions. Each color means something. Intentionally and proactively select colors that will make you feel the way you WANT to feel. The colors you wear impact how you FEEL and how you connect, or don't connect, with others around you.

One outfit tells more than a thousand words!

Personality Based on Color:

Red

Associated with energy, war, danger, strength, power, determination, passion, desire, and love. Enhances human metabolism, increases respiration rate, and raises blood pressure. It attracts attention more than any other color, at times signifying danger.

Colors related to red: Magenta, Burgundy and Maroon

Orange

Combines the energy of red and the happiness of yellow. Associated with joy, sunshine, and the tropics. A personality associated with the color orange is vibrant, energetic, and enthusiastic. They are sociable, adventurous, and spontaneous, with a strong sense of creativity and optimism.

Colors related to orange: Peach, Coral, Rust

Blue

A personality associated with the color blue is calm, dependable, and thoughtful. They are introspective, loyal, and sensitive. Peaceful, flexible and imaginative, they are natural romantics and nurturers.

Colors related to blue: Teal, Turquoise, Aqua

Yellow

Associated with happiness, intellect, and energy. A personality associated with the color yellow is cheerful, optimistic, and energetic. They are creative, sociable, and enthusiastic, often bringing joy, warmth, and positivity to others.

Colors related to yellow: Amber, Beige

Green

A personality associated with the color green is balanced, harmonious, and nurturing. They value stability, and connection, often being practical, empathetic, and supportive. Green symbolizes growth, harmony, freshness, and fertility.

Colors related to green: Olive, Lime, Emerald, Apple

Pink

Pink stands for vulnerability and youth. A personality associated with the color pink is compassionate, affectionate, and caring. They are often nurturing, empathetic, and sensitive, bringing kindness and warmth to relationships.

Colors related to pink: Rose, Blush, Salmon

Purple

Combines the stability of blue and the energy of red. It symbolizes power, nobility, luxury, and ambition. A personality associated with the color purple is imaginative, intuitive, and introspective. They are often creative and spiritual, valuing uniqueness and wisdom.

Colors related to purple: Violet, Lavender, Grape

White

Associated with light, goodness, innocence, purity, and virginity. A personality associated with the color white is pure, organized, and serene. They value simplicity, clarity, and freshness, often being thoughtful, disciplined, and reliable.

Black

A personality associated with the color black is strong, independent, and sophisticated. They are often assertive, introspective, and resilient, valuing elegance, depth, and mystery. Black is considered to be a very formal, elegant, and prestigious color.

Color psychology believes that different colors make us FEEL very different. We can use color therapy to change our feelings, impact our moods and treat depression or sadness. Research has shown that colors can greatly affect our moods and the way other people respond to us.

> *"The best color in the whole world is the one that looks good on you."*
> – Coco Chanel

Purple Creative Imaginative Wise Insightful Charming Powerful	**Light Blue** Freshness Peace Loyalty Calmness Honorable Trustworthy	**Yellow-Gold** Social Optimistic Ambitious Competitive Risk-taker Spontaneous
Yellow Logical Consistent Happy Energetic Intellectual Loyal	**Green** Balanced Optimistic Generous Wisdom Freshness Stability	**Pink** Feminine Romantic Loving Innocent Nurturing Hopeful
Gray Conservative Traditional Serious Mature Modest Functional	**Brown** Dependable Conventional Reliable Comforting Resilient Stable	**Black** Powerful Sophisticated Elegant Authoritative Confident Mysterious
	White Simplicity Humility Precision Kindness Purity Youthful	**Coral/Red** Extroversion Energetic Bold Passionate Strength Intensity

Chapter 09

Color Harmony

Mastering the Art of Outfit Coordination

Color plays an essential role in how we feel and in fashion, as it helps create aesthetically pleasing outfits and influences our emotions. Learn about the power of color with one timeless tool that can transform your wardrobe: the color wheel. Mastering how to match clothes using the color wheel isn't just about following fashion rules; it's about expressing your personality, enhancing your look, and feeling confident in every outfit you wear.

Imagine stepping into your closet and effortlessly pairing pieces that harmonize beautifully, making you feel vibrant and poised. The color wheel is your guide to achieving this effortless elegance. By understanding the relationships between colors you can create visually stunning, harmonious, and striking outfits.

In this chapter, you'll learn how to use the color wheel to your advantage, from creating eye-catching contrasts to crafting subtle, sophisticated palettes. Whether you're aiming for a bold, high-energy look or a soft, serene vibe, the color wheel offers endless possibilities for expressing your unique style.

Get ready to dive into the world of color with confidence. By the end of this chapter, you'll not only master the art of mixing and matching colors effectively but also learn how to make each outfit a true reflection of your personal style. Embrace color coordination as a way to turn your wardrobe into a canvas for creativity and self-expression.

The color wheel is a powerful visual tool that arranges the spectrum of colors in a circular format. It illustrates how colors relate to each other and how they can be combined to create visually pleasing schemes. Here's a simple overview:

THE COLOR WHEEL

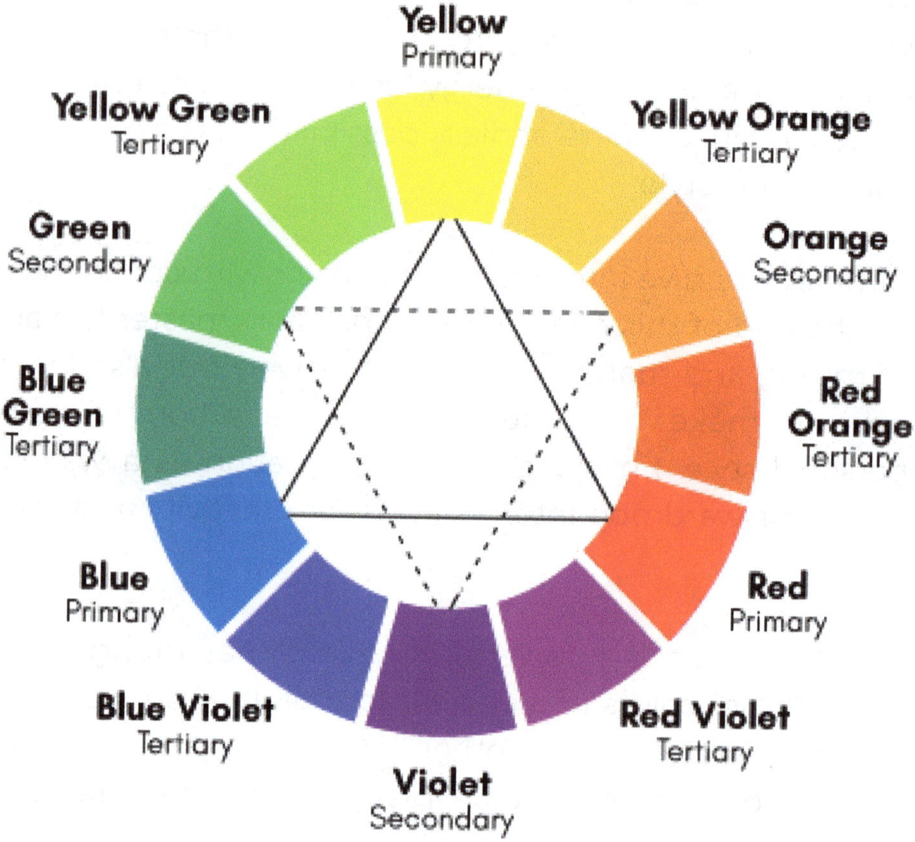

Yellow — Primary
Yellow Orange — Tertiary
Orange — Secondary
Red Orange — Tertiary
Red — Primary
Red Violet — Tertiary
Violet — Secondary
Blue Violet — Tertiary
Blue — Primary
Blue Green — Tertiary
Green — Secondary
Yellow Green — Tertiary

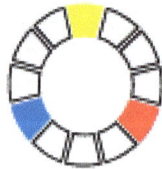

PRIMARY
Yellow
Red
Blue

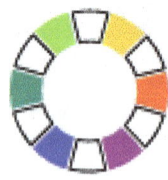

TERTIARY
Yellow Orange
Red Orange
Red Violet
Blue Violet
Blue Green
Yellow Green

SECONDARY
Orange
Violet
Green

Primary colors

First, there are the primary colors. These are the OG colors – red, yellow, and blue. They're the building blocks of every other color on the wheel. Without them, we wouldn't have the beautiful spectrum of hues we know and love.

Secondary colors

Next are secondary colors – green, orange, and purple. These are created by mixing two primary colors together. They're vibrant and playful, perfect for adding a pop of color to your look.

Tertiary colors

Tertiary colors are a bit more complex. These are created by mixing a primary color with a secondary color. Think deep magenta or bright chartreuse. These colors are for the bold and adventurous!

Color temperature

Warm colors

Warm colors are the fiery hues that make you feel alive – red, orange, and yellow. They're perfect for making a statement and showing off your confidence.

Cool colors

On the other hand, cool colors are calm and collected – blue, green, and purple. They give off a peaceful vibe and are perfect for a more subdued look.

Neutral colors

Neutral colors are the backbone of any wardrobe. Black, white, gray, and brown are versatile and can be paired with any other color on the wheel. They're like the glue that holds your outfits together.

So, how do you use the color wheel to create amazing outfits? Look for colors that are next to each other or opposite each other on the wheel. These colors will complement each other and create a cohesive look. Fashion is all about self-expression, so don't be afraid to experiment with different colors and combinations. The possibilities are endless!

When it comes to fashion, color can make all the difference. The color wheel is an essential tool for anyone looking to create visually appealing outfits. But how do you use it effectively? Here are some principles to keep in mind:

Try analogous colors: Analogous colors are colors that are next to each other on the color wheel, such as blue and green. These colors create a harmonious and cohesive look, as they share similar undertones. Consider them neighbors that flow effortlessly. When used together, they create a harmonious and subtle color combination. Analogous colors form relaxing, classy, sophisticated looks. For instance, pairing a blue top with green pants creates a calm and peaceful look. Analogous color outfits are relatively easy to create, as the colors naturally work well together. To create a cohesive look, choose one primary color and use the other colors as accents.

Analogous

You can also try using complementary colors that are opposite each other on the clothing color wheel. These colors create a high-contrast look that is both striking and visually appealing. For example, red and green, blue and orange, or purple and yellow are complementary color pairs. When styling complementary colors, it's crucial to strike a balance between the two contrasting hues. One way to achieve this is by using one color as the dominant shade and the other as an accent. For example, pairing an orange top with green pants creates a strong and vibrant look.

Complementary

Monochromatic color schemes involve using different shades, tints, or tones of a single color. This creates a streamlined and sophisticated look, as the outfit appears to be in perfect harmony. For example, a monochromatic look might include a light blue shirt, a medium blue skirt, and dark blue accessories. When creating a monochromatic look, adding visual interest by incorporating different textures and patterns is essential. For example, you could wear a light blue silk blouse, a medium blue tweed skirt, and dark blue suede pumps. Dressing monochromatically creates a long, lean look.

Monochromatic

Learn to identify warm and cool colors: warm colors create a sense of energy and excitement, while cool colors have a calming effect. Use warm colors to draw attention to a particular area or feature, and cool colors to create a more relaxed look.

And of course, don't forget neutral colors: neutral colors like black, white, gray, and beige are versatile and can be paired with any other color on the wheel. They're perfect for creating a balanced look and can help highlight brighter colors.

Colors play a powerful role in shaping how your figure is perceived, influencing whether you appear taller, shorter, slimmer, or curvier. Dark colors like black, navy, and charcoal have a slimming effect, as they visually recede and minimize certain areas. Conversely, light colors can accentuate or enlarge specific parts. For instance, pairing a light-colored top with dark-colored pants can draw attention to the upper body while creating a slimming effect on the lower half. Embrace the power of color to highlight your best features and craft looks that make you feel confident and radiant.

Color blocking and strategic color placement can work wonders in shaping your figure. Vertical lines and blocks can elongate your silhouette, giving you a taller, slimmer appearance, while horizontal lines and blocks can enhance width or curves. Choosing the right colors and patterns for your body shape can accentuate your natural features and boost your confidence in your clothing choices. For instance, if you have a pear-shaped body, opting for darker colors on the bottom and lighter colors on top can create a more balanced look.

By applying these simple principles, you can create visually appealing and harmonious outfits using the color wheel. Remember, fashion is a form of self-expression, so don't hesitate to experiment with different colors and combinations. Have fun with it and let your unique personality shine through.

"Fashion is about dressing according to what's fashionable. Style is more about being yourself."
– Oscar de la Renta

Chapter 10

Adding a Pop of Color

Simple Tricks to Energize Your Wardrobe

1. Start with analogous colors. Analogous colors are next to each other on the color wheel and share a common hue. When incorporating new colors into your wardrobe, find a color that feels safe to you—for example, light blue. On the color wheel, blue falls between teal and blue-violet. If you feel comfortable with light blue, add on a teal or blue violet for a subtle, two-color palette.

2. Embrace complementary colors. Complementary colors are opposite each other on the color wheel and can make for a beautiful power clash: Think fuchsia and chartreuse, or burgundy and forest green. When you make bold color choices, both colors stand out.

3. Wear accessories that don't "match." Unless you're going for a full monochrome look, don't worry about matching your belt to your handbag and shoes. These smaller accessories are actually a great place to experiment with bright colors.

4. Mix neutral colors. Neutral colors are a great base for working with brighter colors, but they can also work together. Color mixing isn't just about bold colors—neutrals like brown, black, navy blue, and white almost always pair well, so don't be afraid to wear black pants with brown shoes.

5. Wear denim as a neutral color. Consider denim a neutral color, meaning you can mix it with any other color (including blue) and it will probably look great. This also means you can mix denims. The easiest way to do it is with shades of denim that are similar to each other but different enough that your look won't be too matchy. Try pairing mid-wash jeans with a light-wash denim shirt, or dark-wash jeans with a mid-wash denim jacket.

6. Organize your closet according to the color wheel. The simplify process of choosing an outfit by organizing your closet by color. Color-coordinating your closet will make it easier to find exactly what you're looking for, and it will also help you create new color combinations. Grab the piece that you want to wear and hold it up next to the other items in your closet; you'll be able to see which color families work best with your main color.

7. Don't be afraid to try new colors and see how they look on you. You might be surprised at which hues make you feel and look your best.

8. To look your best, select colors that complement your skin undertone.

> *"True beauty radiates not from the skin but from the confidence and joy that come from within. Embrace your skin tone and let your inner light shine."*
> – *Anonymous*

Chapter 11

Tone it Right

Secrets of Skin Undertones

Understanding your skin tone is important when choosing clothes because it helps you select colors that enhance your natural beauty and boost your confidence. Remember, fashion is not just about what you wear, but how it makes you feel. Colors that complement your skin tone can elevate your spirit and highlight your natural beauty. Think of your skin tone as a canvas; choosing the right colors will make your features shine and boost your confidence. When you select colors that work well with your everyday and professional wardrobe, you'll look polished, feel confident, and embrace a stylish presence.

Enhancing Natural Beauty

Complementary Colors: Colors that complement your skin tone can make your complexion look more vibrant and healthier. For instance, if you have a warm skin tone, earthy colors like browns, oranges, and warm reds can highlight your natural glow. Conversely, cooler skin tones are often enhanced by jewel tones, such as emerald green, sapphire blue, and deep purples.

Highlighting Features: The right colors can accentuate your best features. A top or dress in a flattering color can draw attention to your eyes, hair, and overall facial structure, making you look more radiant and polished.

Balancing Undertones: Different skin tones have different undertones, such as yellow, pink, or neutral. Wearing colors that match your undertones can create a harmonious look. For example, warm undertones might look best in gold and yellow shades, while cool undertones might shine in silver and blue hues.

Boosting Confidence

Feeling Good in Your Skin: When you wear colors that suit you, it can make you feel more comfortable and confident. You'll likely receive more compliments and positive feedback, which can boost your self-esteem and overall mood.

Expressing Individuality: Understanding your skin tone allows you to experiment with a palette that reflects your personality. You can create a unique style that feels true to you, enhancing your sense of identity and confidence.

Avoiding Fashion Mistakes: Knowing which colors to avoid can prevent fashion mishaps. For instance, certain colors might make your skin appear washed out or overly red. By steering clear of these shades, you can ensure that your outfits consistently make you look and feel your best.

Consistency in Wardrobe: When you know your ideal color palette, shopping becomes easier and more efficient. You can build a cohesive wardrobe where all pieces work well together, making it easier to mix and match outfits that you know will look great on you.

Understanding your skin tone is key to choosing clothes that enhance your natural beauty and boost your confidence. It empowers you to make fashion choices that truly reflect your unique personality and style, ensuring you feel both comfortable and radiant.

HOW TO FIND YOUR UNDERTONE: 6 DIY TESTS

Finding your undertone can help you choose the best colors for clothing, makeup, and accessories. Here are some simple methods to determine your undertone:

1. The Vein Test

Look at the veins on the inside of your wrist under natural light.

Blue or Purple Veins: You likely have cool undertones.

Green Veins: You likely have warm undertones.

Blue-Green Veins: You may have neutral undertones.

2. The Jewelry Test

Consider whether you look better in gold or silver jewelry.

Silver Jewelry: If silver jewelry looks best on you, you probably have cool undertones.

Gold Jewelry: If gold jewelry looks best on you, you likely have warm undertones.

Both: If both look good, you might have neutral undertones.

3. The White Paper Test

Hold a piece of white paper up to your face and look in a mirror under natural light.

Pink or Bluish Hue: You have cool undertones.

Yellow or Golden Hue: You have warm undertones.

Neither: You may have neutral undertones.

4. The Sun Test

Think about how your skin reacts to the sun.

Burns Easily: If you burn easily and don't tan much, you likely have cool undertones.

Tans Easily: If you can easily and rarely burn, you probably have warm undertones.

5. The Color Test

Hold different colored fabrics or clothing near your face and see which ones look best.

Cool Colors (blues, purples, emeralds): If these colors look best, you have cool undertones.

Warm Colors (yellows, oranges, browns): If these colors suit you better, you have warm undertones.

Both: If both color groups look good, you likely have neutral undertones.

6. Natural Hair and Eye Color

Consider your natural hair and eye color.

Cool Undertones: Typically have blue, gray, or green eyes with blonde, brown, or black hair with ashy tones.

Warm Undertones: Often have brown, amber, or hazel eyes with red, brown, or black hair with golden or red tones.

Neutral Undertones: A mix of these characteristics, not leaning strongly towards cool or warm.

Additional Tips

Foundation Matching: When testing foundations, see which shade blends seamlessly into your skin without leaving a noticeable line.

Avoid Artificial Light: Perform these tests in natural light to get the most accurate result.

By using these methods, you can determine your skin's undertone and make more informed decisions about colors that will complement your natural complexion. Understanding your skin tone is a step toward embracing your unique beauty. Let your wardrobe reflect the masterpiece that you are!

> *"Dressing well is a form of good manners."*
> *– Tom Ford*

Chapter 12

Outfit Magic

Crafting Your Look in Four Simple Steps

Struggling with what to wear and want to look fabulous every time? The secret to effortless style is simpler than you think—just take it one step at a time. Imagine opening your closet and effortlessly assembling an outfit that makes you feel confident and radiant. You're about to discover how easy it can be to unlock the secrets of effortless style and always look and feel your best.

This chapter is designed to simplify the process of creating outfits by breaking it down into four easy, manageable steps. Whether you're looking to revamp your daily wear or need a stylish solution for a special occasion, these steps will help you build a look that's uniquely yours.

By mastering these straightforward steps, you'll acquire the confidence to mix and match pieces effortlessly, ensuring that every outfit showcases your unique style and makes you feel empowered. Say goodbye to wardrobe dilemmas and hello to a closet that seamlessly aligns with you.

Prepare to tap into your inner stylist and experience how simple it can be to create a look that not only complements your style but also boosts your confidence. With "4 Step Outfit Magic," crafting standout outfits will become second nature, turning every day into a chance to shine.

STEP I: Determine how you want to look: Dressy or Casual. Do you want to look casual and wear jeans or pants with a top and flats? Do you want to look dressy and wear a skirt or a dress and heels? Keep this in mind when creating your outfit.

STEP II: Start by picking out one item, which will be your "Base" item, either shoes or clothes. For example, as you are getting ready for the day, you think, "I want to wear my leopard flats to work today" or "I really want to wear that striped sweater." You've got your first piece picked out. If you don't know what you want to start with, pick out a piece in your closet you haven't worn in a while.

If you picked shoes as your base item, patterned shoes (leopard, stripes, floral, etc) look great with solid colors, and solid-colored shoes look great with both solid or patterned clothes.

Solid-Color Shoes

Patterned Shoes

When choosing a top or bottom as a clothing base item. First, choose EITHER a Top or Bottom as your base.

For a Clothing Piece "Base"

If you picked a TOP Solid-color tops look great with a solid-color skirt, pants, jeans or layer it with a sleeveless dress. You can also wear solid-color tops with a patterned bottom piece. If your top is patterned, stick with a solid-color bottom.

If you picked a BOTTOM Solid-color bottoms, like pants, jeans, skirts and leggings, look great with other solid-color tops and patterned tops. If your bottom piece is patterned, then stick with a solid-color top.

Select YOUR SHOES If you have a solid-color top and bottom, you're open to either solid or patterned shoes. If either your top or bottom is patterned, then wear solid-color shoes, like nude or black.

STEP III: Adding a 3rd layer is optional. If the weather permits, wear a 3rd layer. This can be a vest, jacket, poncho, kimono or blazer. By adding a 3rd layer, you instantly add interest to an outfit. This is a great way to add a pop of color to a neutral outfit.

STEP IV: Accessorize your almost complete outfit by adding those final, crucial touches. Fashion accessories fall into two main categories: those that are carried and those that are worn. These elements make an outfit pop and highlight your personal style, taste, and preferences.

Accessories offer endless opportunities to elevate each item you own. You might choose to add a necklace, earrings, and/or a bracelet—wear one or all three! Bold statement jewelry, such as a striking necklace or bracelet, is a major trend. If you enjoy switching handbags daily, ensure each one complements your shoes. Alternatively, swap a necklace for a scarf to add color and flair to a plain outfit. Adding a belt can also create interest and enhance your look.

Accessories

"I like what I see when I am looking at me, when I'm walking past the mirror."
-Mary J. Blige

Chapter 13

Accessorize to Mesmerize

Elevating Your Look with the Perfect Details

Accessories play a crucial role in enhancing outfits and expressing personal style in several significant ways. Now, let's dive into the art of transforming your outfits with the power of accessories. Accessories are not just finishing touches; they are the key to elevating your look from ordinary to extraordinary.

Imagine the impact of a stunning necklace, a bold belt, or a chic scarf—these details have the power to redefine your style and express your personality in ways that go beyond clothing alone. This chapter will show you how to select and style accessories that enhance your wardrobe, making every outfit uniquely yours.

Discover how to choose accessories that enhance your outfits, highlight your best features, and reflect your personal style. From layering jewelry to pairing scarves and shoes, learn how to use accessories to craft dynamic, standout looks that make a lasting impression. With practical tips and inspiring ideas, this chapter will help you unlock the full potential of your accessories, transforming them into powerful tools for style enhancement. Get ready to elevate your wardrobe and captivate with every detail as you master the art of accessorizing.

Completing the Look: Accessories can transform a basic outfit into something polished and complete. They provide the finishing touches that tie together different elements of your clothing.

Adding Personality: Accessories are an excellent way to showcase your personality and individuality. Whether it's through quirky earrings, a statement necklace, or a unique handbag, accessories can communicate your personal style preferences.

Creating Visual Interest: Well-chosen accessories can draw attention to specific parts of your outfit, such as a belt that cinches the waist, statement shoes that pop against a neutral outfit, or a scarf that adds texture and color.

Adapting to Occasions: Accessories allow you to adapt your outfit to different occasions effortlessly. Swapping out accessories allows you to transition from a casual day look to an elegant evening ensemble without changing your entire outfit.

Highlighting Trends: Accessories are often where fashion trends first appear. Incorporating trendy accessories can update your look without needing to overhaul your wardrobe entirely.

Emphasizing Individuality: Accessories provide an opportunity to stand out and express yourself creatively. Mixing and matching accessories allows you to experiment with different styles and create unique combinations that reflect your mood or current trends.

Enhancing Confidence: When you feel good about how you look, your confidence naturally grows. Accessories can enhance this confidence by allowing you to express yourself authentically and stylishly.

Cultural and Symbolic Significance: Some accessories hold cultural or symbolic significance, such as heirloom jewelry or items that commemorate special events. These pieces can carry personal meaning and add depth to your outfit.

Versatility: Accessories are versatile and can be reused in various ways. A single accessory, like a scarf or a pair of sunglasses, can be styled in multiple ways to create different looks.

Attention to Detail: Accessories demonstrate attention to detail and show that you've put thought into your appearance. They can elevate a simple outfit into a sophisticated ensemble that leaves a lasting impression.

Accessories are essential not only for enhancing the visual appeal of your outfits but also for expressing your unique identity and style. They offer a creative outlet for experimentation and allow you to adapt your look to different settings and occasions effortlessly. Selecting and styling the right accessories, such as jewelry, scarves, bags, and shoes, can greatly enhance your outfit. Here's a quick guide to help you choose and style these accessories effectively:

Jewelry Definition: Personal ornaments, such as necklaces, rings, or bracelets, that are typically made from or contain jewels and precious metal.

Jewelry Selection

Consider Your Outfit: Choose jewelry that complements the neckline and style of your clothing. For example, a pendant necklace goes well with V-neck tops, while statement earrings can highlight a simple dress.

Metal Tones: Match jewelry metals with the overall tone of your outfit. For cool tones (blues, purples), opt for silver or white gold; for warm tones (reds, yellows), choose gold or rose gold.

Occasion: Adjust the size and type of jewelry based on the occasion. Delicate pieces for formal events, bold pieces for casual outings.

Personal Style: Reflect your personality with jewelry choices. If you prefer minimalist looks, opt for simple studs or delicate chains; for a bolder style, choose chunky bracelets or statement rings.

Jewelry Styling

Layering: Experiment with layering different lengths of necklaces for a trendy look. Mix metals and textures (e.g., pearls with chains) for added interest.

Balance: If you wear statement earrings, go easy on other jewelry pieces to avoid overwhelming your look. Balance larger pieces with smaller, complementary ones.

Rings and Bracelets: Coordinate rings with your outfit; stack rings for a modern look or wear a statement ring as a focal point. Mix and match bracelets for a layered effect, but avoid overcrowding your wrists.

Scarf Definition: A length or square of fabric worn around the neck or head.

Scarf Selection

Material: Choose scarves based on the season—lightweight fabrics like silk or cotton for spring/summer, and wool or cashmere for fall/winter.

Pattern and Color: Coordinate scarves with your outfit's color palette. Use scarves to add a pop of color or introduce patterns (stripes, florals) that complement your clothing.

Size and Shape: Consider the size and shape of the scarf—longer scarves are versatile for different tying techniques, while square scarves can be folded into different styles.

Scarf Styling

Neck Scarves: Tie around your neck in various styles—loop through, knot loosely, or tie in a bow—to add a chic touch to blouses or dresses.

Headscarves: Wear as a headband, turban, or wrap around a ponytail for a playful or sophisticated look.

Belt or Bag Accessory: Use scarves as a belt substitute around your waist or tie onto your handbag for added flair.

Bag Definition: Often made of leather, fabric, plastic, or the like, held in the hand or carried by means of a handle or strap, commonly used for holding money, personal grooming items, small purchases, etc.

Bag Selection

Size and Functionality: Choose a bag size that suits your needs (small clutch for evenings, tote for daily use). Ensure it complements your outfit's proportions.

Color and Material: Opt for versatile colors (black, tan, navy) that coordinate with multiple outfits. Consider leather for durability or canvas for casual settings.

Hardware: Pay attention to bag hardware (buckles, zippers, studs). Match metals with your jewelry for a cohesive look.

Bag Styling

Occasion: Select bags appropriate for the occasion—formal events call for elegant clutches, while cross body bags are practical for everyday use.

Coordinate: Match your bag with your shoes for a polished appearance. Alternatively, contrast colors or textures for a more eclectic style.

Carry Style: Experiment with different ways of carrying your bag—handheld, on the shoulder, cross body—to suit your outfit and comfort level.

Shoe Selection

Comfort: Prioritize comfort alongside style. Choose shoes that you can wear comfortably for the occasion.

Style: Select shoes that complement your outfit's formality—flats or loafers for casual looks, heels or boots for dressier occasions.

Color: Coordinate shoe color with your outfit—match or contrast for visual interest.

Shoe Styling

Balance: Ensure shoes complement your outfit's proportions. For example, ankle boots pair well with skinny jeans or dresses, while delicate sandals suit flowing skirts or cropped pants.

Pop of Color: Use shoes as a statement piece by opting for bold colors or patterns that draw attention to your feet.

Seasonal Adaptation: Choose shoes appropriate for the season—sandals for summer, ankle boots for fall, and boots for winter—to complement your overall look.

General Tips

Less is More: Avoid overwhelming your outfit with too many accessories. Choose a few key pieces to highlight.

Experiment: Don't be afraid to try new combinations and styles. Accessories are a great way to experiment with trends and showcase your personal flair.

Mirror Check: Before heading out, do a quick mirror check to ensure your accessories complement your outfit and overall look cohesive.

By following these guidelines, you can effectively select and style accessories to enhance your outfits while expressing your personal style with confidence.

Accessorizing is all about balance and enhancing your outfit without overpowering it. Here are some tips to accessorize effectively:

- **Focus on a Few Statement Pieces:** Select one or two standout accessories, like a bold necklace or a patterned scarf, and let them shine. Keep other accessories subtle to avoid competing focal points.
- **Match Metals:** If you're wearing silver jewelry, stick with silver-toned accessories like belt buckles or shoe accents. Consistency in metal tones creates a cohesive look.
- **Consider Proportions:** If you're wearing a busy pattern or detailed clothing, opt for simpler accessories. Conversely, if your outfit is minimalistic, you can go for more elaborate pieces.
- **Balance Colors:** Accessories should complement your outfit's color scheme. Choose accessories in colors that either match or complement your clothes rather than clash with them.

- **Layer Wisely:** Layering accessories can add depth to your outfit but be mindful not to overdo it. For example, if you're wearing a statement necklace, pair it with simpler earrings rather than adding more layers.
- **Don't Forget Functionality:** Accessories should also serve a purpose. For instance, a belt can define your waistline while adding a stylish touch, or a scarf can keep you warm while adding a pop of color.
- **Consider the Occasion:** Tailor your accessories to the occasion. For formal events, opt for classic pieces like pearls or a sleek watch. For casual outings, experiment with more playful or relaxed accessories.
- **Personalize:** Use accessories to showcase your personal style. Whether it's a favorite ring, a sentimental bracelet, or a unique brooch, incorporating pieces that reflect your personality adds authenticity to your look.
- **Less is More:** Sometimes, simplicity is key. If you're unsure about an accessory, it's often better to skip it than risk overwhelming your outfit.
- **Experiment and Adjust:** Try different combinations and see what works best for you. Don't be afraid to adjust or remove accessories until you find the right balance that enhances your outfit without overshadowing it.

By following these tips, you can effectively accessorize to complement your outfit and create a polished, cohesive look.

A few more tips for creating a fabulous outfit:

Find your own personal style: Discover what colors look best with your skin tone. Decide what style of dresses, skirts, pants and tops flatter your figure. Stick with those.

Plan Ahead: Don't wait until you are getting ready to go out to choose your outfit. Set aside time to plan outfits that you want to wear. Take a picture so you will remember.

Organize Your Closet: So that you only see items that fit and you want to wear.

Contrast: Clothes look great when there is contrast. If you're wearing a light-colored top, then wear a darker bottom. Examples: white tee and indigo or colored jeans, striped top and solid-color bottom, dark-colored top and light-colored pants.

Layers: Layers create interest in an outfit and make the outfit look complete.

Matching Accessories: If your outfit is simple, say a white tee and jeans, match the color of your handbag and shoes. Your outfit will look "put together" every time.

Matching Metals: If you wear gold jewelry, a good idea is for the hardware on your handbag and/or shoes is the same. Same for silver jewelry.

Shoe Color: Black and Nude shoes go well with almost any outfit. Patterned shoes (leopard, stripes, flowers) go well with solid-color outfits.

Pinterest: Look for outfit ideas on Pinterest. You can do searches like "plaid shirt," "skinny jeans," or "pencil skirt," and it will display outfit ideas. You can even create a board for your outfit ideas!

Step Outside of Your Comfort Zone: Add a color or item that you usually would not wear to an outfit.

Ask for Help: If you see someone who always looks great, tell them and ask for ideas. People who are stylish usually love to talk about clothes and would be happy to help.

SMILE: It makes anything you wear look even better!

Reflect, Reveal, Renew

What three words do you want others to use when describing your style? How can you incorporate these words into your wardrobe?

_____
_____
_____
_____
_____
_____
_____
_____
_____
_____
_____
_____
_____
_____
_____
_____
_____
_____
_____
_____
_____

Think back to a time when you felt your most confident and comfortable in your clothing. What elements of that outfit contributed to making you feel this way?

___

Browse through your favorite fashion magazines or Pinterest boards. What recurring themes, colors, or styles do you notice? How can you integrate these into your personal wardrobe?

Think about your lifestyle and daily activities. What clothing choices would best support your routines while still expressing your individuality?

_____
_____
_____
_____
_____
_____
_____
_____
_____
_____
_____
_____
_____
_____
_____
_____
_____
_____
_____
_____
_____
_____
_____
_____
_____
_____
_____

Write about a fashion icon or someone whose style you admire. What aspects of their style resonate with you, and how can you adapt these elements to fit your personal taste?

_____
_____
_____
_____
_____
_____
_____
_____
_____
_____
_____
_____
_____
_____
_____
_____
_____
_____
_____
_____

Clutter is not just the stuff on your floor—it's anything that stands between you and the life you want to be living."
– Peter Walsh

Chapter 14

Neat Closets, Happy Minds

The Mental Health Benefits of Organization

Imagine opening your closet and hearing a choir of angels. That's right, no more wrestling with unruly hangers or dodging a cascade of falling clothes. Welcome to the ZEN of an organized closet, where mental health gets a stylish upgrade! Here are some ways the organization of your closet can have a surprisingly significant impact on your mental health.

Reduced Stress and Anxiety

A cluttered closet can lead to both visual and mental clutter. The constant sight of disorganized items can elevate stress levels and create feelings of overwhelm. An organized closet makes it easier to find what you need, reducing frustration and the anxiety of searching for misplaced items. When your closet resembles a neatly arranged boutique, finding your favorite shirt no longer feels like an archaeological dig. Say goodbye to frantic, stress-filled mornings and hello to calm, coffee-sipping moments.

Sense of Accomplishment

Organizing your closet can give you a tangible sense of achievement. Completing such a task can boost your mood and provide a feeling of control over your environment. A neat and organized closet can create a more pleasant and calming atmosphere, which can positively influence your overall mood. Tackling that mess of clothes and turning it into a Pinterest-worthy space feels like winning a small, stylish victory. It's a daily reminder that you've got this adulting thing down. Plus, now you have a legitimate reason to reward yourself with more clothes!

Enhanced Productivity

Efficiency: An organized closet can streamline your daily routines, saving time in the morning and reducing the stress of decision-making. This efficiency can contribute to a more productive day and a better overall mood. With a well-organized closet, choosing what to wear becomes simpler and quicker, reducing decision fatigue and conserving mental energy.

Improved Self-Esteem

Managing and organizing your space can contribute to a more positive self-image. Feeling that you have control over your environment can reinforce feelings of competence and self-worth. When your clothes are organized, you may feel more excited about your wardrobe, leading to better self-esteem and confidence.

Increased Calmness and Relaxation

Stress Reduction: An organized closet can lead to a more serene and orderly living space, which can enhance relaxation and reduce feelings of stress. Creating a mindful and intentional space, even in a closet, can contribute to overall mental tranquility. There's something oddly satisfying about a well-organized closet. It's like feng shui for your wardrobe, bringing a sense of peace and tranquility to your space. Instead of avoiding your closet like a haunted house, you might just find yourself admiring it for fun.

Clarity and Focus

A tidy closet is like a well-organized brain. No more wasting precious mental energy deciding between that old concert tee or the shirt you actually do like. Everything is in its place, leaving your mind clear for more important decisions—like what to have for lunch.

Confidence Boost

Ever notice how an outfit that's easy to find can make you feel like you've got your life together? An organized closet means you'll always know where your best pieces are, helping you strut out the door with confidence. Who knew a tidy closet could double as a pep talk?

Enhanced Routine and Structure

Consistent Habits: An organized closet can support consistent daily routines, which can be especially helpful for those managing mental health conditions like anxiety or depression. Having a predictable and orderly closet can add a sense of stability and control to your day.

Organization isn't just about tidiness; it's about creating a space that fosters clarity, efficiency, and peace of mind."
– Anonymous

Chapter 15

Clear the Closet Chaos

Now that you've learned how to choose the right colors and know your signature style, it's time to clear out what you don't need or wear to make space for what you truly desire. Cleaning out your closet can be an emotional journey, but to create a wardrobe that truly serves you, letting go of excess is essential. Holding onto unnecessary items will only slow down the process. Before you start purging, ask yourself, "What are my day-to-day wardrobe needs?" Keep this in mind as you sort through your closet. For example, if you're a stay-at-home new mom, you might need to reconsider the number of 5-inch heels in your closet, as you'll likely be chasing after a toddler for the next few years.

Here are some simple techniques you can use:

Create time for it.

Set a specific time for the task. You can do it in bits throughout the week or set aside a few hours on a Saturday. Consider your closet size and daily schedules.

Consider your weight.

Have clothes that fit you, not clothes that are too small in hopes that you will wear them when you lose weight or clothes that are too big, and you keep saying you will re-size them, but you never do.

Think about your daily activities.

Consider where you go every day and dress based on the events and places you spend most of your time. Remove everything from your closet and create three piles. Go through every item and place it in a heap. Ask questions like;

- Does it fit?
- Is it stained, damaged, torn, or faded?
- Do I like it now?
- When and where will I wear this?

Separate things into Keep, Donate/Sell, or Throw Away. Use the 80/20 rule when tidying your closet. The 80/20 rule suggests that we use or wear 20% of our things roughly 80% of the time. Since we usually wear 20% of our clothes or shoes 80% of the time, you can purge a significant amount of them. Avoid "What Ifs" and be ruthless. Get rid of anything unworn in a year, things in bad shape, and those items that don't fit anymore.

Stick to a color palette of your favorite colors that look best on you.

What looks best on you? Essentially, anything more than five is not OK regarding color palettes. Purge off-the-scheme colors and stick to your top five hues. Blending colors produces multiple outfit and accessory ideas and gives room for mixing and matching. You can use the online color wheel apps and charts to discover unexpected ways to combine different colors.

Identify the most versatile essentials in your closet.

As you sort through your items, identify the essentials—your staples—such as slacks, dresses, coats, sweaters, tops, and statement jewelry. These will form the foundation of many outfits. Set aside anything that makes you look (and feel!) elegant throughout the day.

Tips For Choosing Essentials.

Your essentials should be timeless and trend-proof. Casual tops with sleeves, t-shirts, vests, and a few dressy blouses/shirts to wear with pants, skirts, and boots. Sticking to classic designs is better than following trends.

Capitalize on good-quality pieces and simple colors. Neutral colors like black, ivory, dark blue, and white allow you to mix and match them quickly when layering. Neutral-colored knitwear and button-down cardigans blend well with casual tops and shirts and come in handy in unpredictable weather.

Remember to set aside shoes and clothing items needing repair or alterations and make the necessary appointments within the next couple of weeks.

Organize Your Closet.

Add some drawer shelves or buy closet organizers to make your wardrobe more efficient and accessible. For instance, have one drawer for sweaters and another for underclothes, T-shirts, dresses, etc., so they are easier to find when needed.

It is best if you can arrange your wardrobe by colors.

You can also keep your closet streamlined by storing pieces out of season somewhere else, like in storage bins.

Once you finish purging, you may notice you need a thing or two. It is time to go shopping!

Summary of Practical Tips for Closet Organization

Declutter Regularly: Periodically review your wardrobe and remove items that are no longer needed or that don't bring you joy. This helps maintain a sense of order.

Categorize Items: Group similar items together, such as shirts, pants, or seasonal clothing. This makes finding what you need quicker and easier.

Utilize Storage Solutions: Invest in storage solutions like bins, shelves, or dividers to keep items organized and accessible.

Maintain Consistency: Develop and stick to a system for organizing your closet to keep it orderly over time.

Create a Routine: Make closet organization a regular part of your routine to prevent clutter from building up.

By addressing closet organization, you can create a more orderly and calming environment, which contributes positively to your overall mental health and well-being. So, embrace the joy of a decluttered closet. Not only will it make getting dressed a breeze, but it'll also give your mental health a fabulous makeover. Who knew closet organization could be the ultimate self-care hack?

As we close the pages of "Dress Better, Feel Better: Unlocking the Power of Clothing to Elevate Your Mood and Boost Your Confidence," remember that the journey of transformation is as much about the inner self as it is about the outer appearance. Your wardrobe is not merely a collection of garments; it is a reflection of your identity, a tool for empowerment and a canvas for your personal expression.

Throughout this book, we've explored the profound impact that a thoughtfully curated wardrobe can have on your confidence, mood, and overall outlook on life. From discovering your personal style and choosing colors that enhance your skin tone to decluttering and organizing your closet, each step has been a journey toward not just looking good, but feeling great.

As you embark on this journey of wardrobe transformation, take with you the knowledge that what you wear is a statement of who you are and who you aspire to be. Allow each outfit to be a celebration of your unique story, and let your personal style be a reflection of your most authentic self.

The true essence of this transformation lies in how you perceive yourself and how you embrace the power of change. By dressing in a way that makes you feel confident and aligned with your true self, you are setting the stage for a life filled with greater self-assurance, joy, and fulfillment.

So, as you step into your newly transformed wardrobe, carry with you the knowledge that change is not just about clothes but about embracing the best version of yourself. Dress better, feel better, and let this transformation remind you of the incredible power you have to shape your life and future.

Thank you for joining me on this journey. Here's to your ongoing transformation and to a life where you not only dress with intention but also live with purpose and confidence.

About The Author

Kelli Stenhouse is a multifaceted professional dedicated to helping others unlock their fullest potential. With a rich background as an educator, human resources administrator, and image consultant, Kelli brings a unique blend of expertise to the table and has spent years guiding individuals through personal and professional growth. Serving as mentor, coach and motivational speaker, she inspires others to navigate difficult transitions and embrace change with confidence. Passionate about the power of appearance and self-presentation, she believes that everyone has the potential to shine and is committed to providing the tools and insights needed to achieve that brilliance.

www.ingramcontent.com/pod-product-compliance
Lightning Source LLC
Chambersburg PA
CBHW070847160426
43192CB00012B/2335